GOD'S THEME PARK OF LIFE

C. Clay Westby

Copyright © 2017 by C. Clay Westby
Library of Congress Control Number: 2018941057

ISBN 978-1-4958-2089-2 paperback
ISBN 978-1-4958-2090-8 eBook

Printed in the United States of America

Published December 2017

INFINITY PUBLISHING
1094 New DeHaven Street, Suite 100
West Conshohocken, PA 19428-2713
Toll-free (877) BUY BOOK
Local Phone (610) 941-9999
Fax (610) 941-9959
Info@buybooksontheweb.com
www.buybooksontheweb.com

This book is dedicated to my beautiful wife, Lynn,
and my children, Kaila and Craig.

Acknowledgments

Special thanks to my mother, Donna Westby, who assisted me in the editing process. I love my mother beyond words!

I would also like to thank family, friends and especially my Aunt Kathy, for previewing parts of my book. I appreciated all of their support, comments, and opinions.

Illustrators for this book were my nephews, Elliot and Levi. Robert, their father, drew the rainbow. Their artistic talent is much appreciated.

Contents for

GOD'S THEME PARK OF LIFE
PARK TRAINING MANUAL.

At the beginning of each life lesson there is a rule, or maybe just a thought. At the end of the lessons, there will be quotes for you to ponder.

Preface

With the exception of the work that is quoted or prefaced in some way; this book is based upon my thoughts, experiences, observations, and perceptions. The thing about writing this book is that the words that fill the following pages will get analyzed, critiqued, dissected, and examined. It is a given that some, but certainly not all of the views or opinions contained in this book have previously found their way to ink and paper. If any human error was made regarding anything in this book, please do not hesitate for one moment, to go directly to God, and let Him know that you forgive me!

I am hopeful, that in some way, the words that are between the front and back cover of this book will jump out at you, and affect you in a positive way. By writing this book I developed an individual and personal relationship with God that makes sense to me, and works for me in many ways. I am hopeful, that after you read this book, you will have a basis from which you can develop an individual and personal relationship with God that makes sense to you, and works in your life.

We all have questions about this world, and about our own life. We start with, what is the meaning of life? And we continue with questions like: Why did this, that, or the other thing, happen to me, you, or them?

Before reading this book, I would like you to read the following sentences, and fully understand their meanings:

THERE IS NO MYSTERY, ABOUT THE FACT THAT LIFE IS A MYSTERY!

GOD IS BEYOND ALL HUMAN UNDERSTANDING AND COMPREHENSION!

Now that you have read, and comprehended both sentences, we can move on.

It is hoped that during the reading of this book, you will interpret things in your own way, believe in God in your own way, praise God in your own way, and love God in your own way. By doing it your way, you can have a personal meaningful relationship with, OUR ONE GOD.

Before you leave the preface area, I think I had better talk to you a little bit about how this book is set up. This book is actually a training manual for all of those individuals who visit God's Theme Park of Life. I thought it best to give everyone the opportunity to read this Park Training Manual, because of all the inherent dangers that are actually a part of this park.

There are 19 lessons to go through, and once a person has completed all of the training, he or she will be better prepared to enter the park. It is in your own best interest to read all of the lessons. Really! Seriously! Whatever you do, do not enter the park by jumping to the last pages of this book! Don't let God hear any integrity, honor, or character warning bells! I guess if you feel that the whole reading policy is a negative thing, then I should let you know that the positive in all this, is that there are no tests or quizzes in any of the lessons.

Let me guess; you're probably wondering why on earth do you have to read a training manual, before you visit a theme park? Was I right? Well, to answer your question, I need you to start lesson 1, and proceed through lesson 19. While the pages lead you to God's Theme Park of Life, the words on the pages will transcend into your thoughts. When you enter God's Theme Park of Life you will have your answer, even if you forget your question. Thanks for your cooperation. The park management also thanks you.

Oh, one more thing, before you start the first lesson, I should tell you, that it is your thoughts, and not my thoughts, that are important to you, and your relationship with God. So, during the lessons, I encourage you to agree, or disagree with any of my thoughts. After each lesson, you can share all of your thoughts with God. I know God will enjoy your company.

Lesson 1................. Sun Life

THOUGHT: Sometimes you have to just sit back and take it all in...

Our Planet Earth is a ball of matter that is in constant motion as it rotates around the sun. Out beyond earth is space, and it goes on... and on... and on... We can only assume that space has no beginning, or end.

The sun in our sky creates light for our day. When the sun fades away, and blackness takes its place, our moon is then able to capture the light from the now missing sun. This moon looms above us, along with the stars, providing light amidst all of the darkness. When the sun reappears, another day begins, and time advances one more day.

MORE THAN MANY DAYS HAVE COME AND GONE! In fact, earth has existed for four and a half billion years. Historically speaking; based on our current calendar, and when my book was published, there had been 2,017 years of life on earth pretty much accounted for, and documented, in many different ways. It's just the other 4,499,997,983 years, before our current calendar started, that we have questions about.

We live on earth, and explore what earth has to offer us. We look up, and bend our minds as to the possibilities of what space also has to offer us; not that our minds aren't already twisted in knots from thinking about how we came to be. How we came to be, and how we are allowed to exist, is only by the grace of God.

Very little is known about space and what lies beyond our planet. At this time, it is still unknown if life exists somewhere far away. For reasons, unknown to us, life is a part of earth as light is a part of the sun.

The sun keeps our planet alive by providing us with light, and heat. But does the average person ever take the time to even think about the sun, as far as how important it is to our daily lives here on Planet Earth? For most of us, the sun serves only as a reminder that we need to put on our sun-block, and our sunglasses.

The earth, sun, and moon are in constant motion. The earth spins and moves around an average size star that is called the sun. The sun is the closest star to earth. The term closest, which is the opposite of farthest, loses something in the meaning when you stop to realize that the earth is around 93,000,000 miles away from the sun. This ball of fire has a diameter of around 900,000 miles, while the earth only has a diameter of around 8,000 miles.

The moon, not being a star, or a planet, is called a moon, because that is what it is, a moon. While Planet Earth moves around the sun, the moon circles the earth.

Before I even started to think about writing this book, I found myself on a hillside near day's end, with random thoughts filling my mind, but yet, still not really thinking about anything; just outside enjoying the day. Looking up, I saw the sun, with all its radiant color, and noticed the outline of the moon beyond the floating white clouds, and the picturesque blue sky. As the wind, or natural forces made the clouds pass by, I pondered about the vastness of it all... and then BAM! It hit me; not like a ton of bricks or anything, but that we are on a spinning ball shaped macrocosm, which continues to travel around the sun, in a perfect life-giving way. Since that one day on the hillside, I look up a lot, you know, taking it all in; everything from the moon and the stars, to Planet Earth and God!

Just clear your mind, take a relaxing breath, and think about the awesomeness of our world!

--- C.W.

"From now until the end of time, no one else will ever see life with my eyes, and I mean to make the most of my chance."

--- Christopher Morley (2)

"Don't go to the grave with life unused."

--- Bobby Bowden (2)

Lesson 2..............Life's Start

RULE: Don't get all stressed out thinking about the beginning. At this point, the ending is what matters the most!

God created this specific planet with the ultimate goal of giving people, who were made in His image, a place to experience life. He did it by the POWER OF GOD, and created all things in a matter of a week, or He did it by the POWER OF GOD, and allowed evolution to progress, or He...............

Creationism:

"In the beginning, God created the heavens and the earth." On the first day God created "light." On the second day God created the "sky." On the third day God created "land" with "seed bearing plants" and "trees;" He also created the "seas." On day four God created the "sun," the "moon," and the "stars." On day five God said: "Let the waters swarm with fish and other life;" and He also said: "Let the skies be filled with birds of every kind." On day six God said: "Let the earth bring forth every kind of animal;" and "God created people in His own image." On day seven, "God rested from all of His work." "And God blessed the seventh day and declared it holy." ---- Genesis 1(3)

7 days! As humans, it is very hard to accept the possibility that God made this world in just six days, and rested on the seventh day. Is it possible that God's time table then, was different than ours is now? In order to even accept that creationism is true, one would have to let go of human logic, and just go on faith alone; and maybe that's what God wants.

Creationism plugs into the seven-day week rather well; which tells me that God likes us to work, but He also wants us to take some time to remember Him. God showed us that on the seventh day He rested, so maybe it would be a good idea for all of us, to take time out of our busy week, to relax and reflect on God, the world, our families and our own personal lives.

The following is a very simplistic, evolutionary, narrative time line. The years noted in this paragraph are definitely not exact, but they are not wild crazy guesses either; or are they?

The earth got its start 4.50 billion years ago. Less than a billion years passed by when simple cell organisms popped up. Another half a billion years went by before photosynthesis became a part of the earth. 2 billion years ago, complex organisms appeared. After another billion years went by, multi-cellular life, in one form or another, sprang up. Later, simple animals showed up, and just over 500 million years ago, there was an onset of complex animals. 475 million years ago, plants sprouted up on land. Approximately two hundred million years came and went until earth saw the emergence of the dinosaurs. By the time the 150-million-year mark rolled around mammals were running around on land, and birds were flapping their wings in the sky. 65 million years ago the dinosaurs ceased to exist! Over sixty million years passed before a species, related to man, was introduced to earth; about 2.50 million years ago. Around 200,000 BC, humans, who kind of looked like you and me, arrived on the scene. If God did make our world by way of evolution, it's very apparent that it took a whole lot longer than a week!

It is possible, that man, from the beginning of time, followed the natural course of evolution. God, however, may have stepped in from the project He was already working on, earth, to create a modern man and woman, in His unique and Godly way.

Throughout earth's long history there have been many ice ages and volcanic events, along with geological movements, and astronomical happenings. After each natural occurrence, life ended, life survived, and life evolved. The earth has not stopped evolving, and it continues to evolve today.

Based on fossil evidence, and carbon dating, the theory of evolution is an accepted theory by many. It appears that all of the natural phenomena, happened in the order that they did, and the way that they did, so Planet Earth would develop into a living planet; a planet that humans can not only live on, but also rule over. I am not so sure, it could even be possible, for nature to be so perfect, but, yet with God, anything is possible!

Our time consists of seconds, minutes, hours, days, months, and years, which is a human concept. Evolution, is a word, that scientists use to explain things in human terms. Guess, what? God created this world, in His own time, and on His own terms!

Possible answers to the start of life: God and evolution, or God and creationism, or possibly, even a little of both! The exciting thing about all this, is that creationism and evolution have the same starting point, and that starting point is God.

When you factor in everything unknown to us, but known to God, then you just have to trust in God. God knows how the world was made, and that's good enough for me.

It seems, lately, that a day goes by like a snap of a finger, and Christmas is always just around the corner. Time is one of those things that just keeps on going, and going, and going. So much time has passed by since the beginning of our world that none of us will ever know all of the answers to our past; heck, we probably don't even know all of the questions! There is no debate about the fact, that there was a beginning for Planet Earth, so it stands to reason that there will be an ending. The Bible already has a name for it, it's called Judgment Day.

For me, personally, I'm going to leave the past in the past, and get myself lined up and squared away for Judgment Day. Given the choice between heaven and hell, I choose all of eternity in heaven; thank you very much!

So, nature, without any prompting from God, just happened to make the right oxygen level, the right climate, the right resources that gave us the means to have an industrial revolution, the right seeds for planting, the right soil for growing things, the right foods to eat, the right water sources, and other miscellaneous resources. And nature also made the earth the right distance from the sun, the moon, and the stars, and made this, that, and the other thing so perfectly... Right!... Sure it did... NOT!!!

--- C.W.

Life is a mystery... there, I hope I cleared that up for you!

--- C.W.

"Yesterday is History
Tomorrow is a Mystery
Today is a Gift
That's why they call it
The Present."

--- unknown author

It is hard for us to envision eternity. Days end, months end, years end, but ETERNAL EXISTENCE...... Never Ends!!

--- C.W.

Lesson 3......... Physical Life

THOUGHT: Heavenly Beings are perfect, and human beings are not.

The actual physical body and brain that make up a human being are beyond magnificent, in and of themselves. The way everything works or functions, and the way the brain and body work collectively together, is truly amazing. Looking at what we are, physically, from the tips of our toes, to the tops of our heads, we find that we are truly an astonishing and unique species. The intangibles about a person are even more spectacular: Thinking and reasoning abilities, thoughts, imagination, and so much more. I am guessing here, but there must be a gazillion things that make up a human body, so pretty much, unfortunately, a gazillion things can go wrong with it too.

The human body, which includes the brain, being physical in nature, can get sick with diseases, break down, stop functioning, and die. The causes for these attacks on the human body are genetic, environmental, self- inflicted, and random. A lot of the time, there is no rhyme or reason as to why some humans have problems, and other humans do not. Remember, HEAVENLY BEINGS ARE PERFECT, AND HUMAN BEINGS ARE NOT!

The health of any human can start out bad, and end bad, but it can also start out good, and end good too. Being a still born baby is a bad day for any human being. Dying younger than most, and in pain, is also going to be a bad time for anyone. Making it through that first day alive, and living a long and wonderful life, until a day comes when one dies in their sleep, is what most people at least hope for.

In between the beginning and end of this life and death continuum, there are a number of human beings, who for one reason or another, have to cope with pain and suffering; some for a short period of time, others for a long period of time, and still others for their entire human life. Human beings can even have physical challenges, or mental challenges. I could go on and on, but I think I have scared myself enough, to the point that I just want to go hide in a corner, and throw a blanket over my head. Then I realize that there are a lot of people who enjoy this world for a period of time with brains and bodies that are pretty much unscathed.

As the candles on a birthday cake take up more space, age related maladies may arise. A well-lit birthday cake, may even imply that many birthday wishes have come true. When blowing out the candles, one can reflect on the life already lived, and wonder about the life that is yet to come.

If mental or physical problems enter the picture, humans often ask questions such as: "Why did that happen to me, you, us, him, her, or them?" "Why does God allow some to suffer, and others not to suffer?" When Jesus was being treated inhumanely, suffering, and dying on the cross, Jesus uttered the words: "My God, my God, why have you forsaken me?" ---- Matthew 27(3)

When Jesus was on the cross, calling out to God, He was in His human form. Nowadays, there are an unending number of humans, all calling out to God in times of crises. And, not all of the calls, are "health" related. In fact, there is always a big up-swing, in the amount of calls, when disasters, natural or otherwise occur.

It is possible, and in my mind probable, that for periods of time, God's plans, just allow the world to exist; and what happens in the world, or to a person, is just a part of life away from heaven. If this is the case, I would imagine that God wants all of us, to be happy, and have joy in our hearts; while He allows us to work out the details of His plans. Did you notice, that I didn't say "all" of the details?!

In the case of Jesus Christ, God had not forgotten about Jesus dying on the cross. God had a plan, and He just wanted it to play out. Lucky for us, it did; as you will see in the very next lesson! In the case of the human race, God has not forgotten about us either, and His plans for us, are still playing out. Exciting, Isn't it?! I love a good mystery! I hope you like a good mystery too, since God sure does like to work in mysterious ways. Could it be, that angels, are one of those mysterious ways?

I will be the first to admit, that I got a little sidetracked, with a thought or two. Now, to conclude this Physical Life Lesson, I will just say, that God wants us to be on earth, for only a period of time; so ultimately, we will join Him in heaven, where we will all have perfect heavenly bodies. By having imperfect bodies on earth, isn't that a motivator to want to go to heaven?

"Success; it is what you do with what you've got."
--- Woody Hayes (2)

"Make the most of yourself, for that is all there is to you."
--- Emerson (2)

18

Lesson 4............. Gift of Life

RULE: Believe in God the Father, God the Son, and God the Holy Spirit. Believe that Jesus died on a cross for our sins, and gave us baptism for our redemption.

God, understanding all, wanted to show us how much He loved us. He wanted to give a special gift to the entire human race; those that lived on earth in the past, the present, and in the future. God was actually going to put us before Himself. God knew that this would only be possible by way of an ultimate sacrifice. This is why God had His son leave His side, and become human for a period of time.

God's son (Jesus) walked the earth as a human being, experiencing life in a physical body. He was able to taste, touch, hear, feel, and see. Jesus, (God) the man, with (God), the Holy Spirit, stayed true to Himself, true to His Father, (God), and true to mankind. He completed the many things that He was sent to earth to do, without committing a sin. He gave us knowledge about God, faith, and spiritual direction.

When the time was right, God implemented His plan to save all human beings from their sins. He did this, when He gave us a Godly gift, and allowed His only son to die on a cross as a human being, for human beings, so all of mankind's past, present, and future sins could be forgiven. Knowing that if He sacrificed His own son, all would know how much He truly loves us.

When Jesus, was dying on the cross for our salvation; Jesus, in His human form, had to endure all of the pain, wretchedness, and suffering that went with it. Three days after Jesus' human body died on the cross, He rose from the dead, and ascended into God's Heavenly Kingdom.

Our omnipotent and wonderful God did not have to do any of this; but He did. He especially did not have to have His son leave His Heavenly Kingdom, to become human, and die a very humiliating human death; but He did. This all-powerful God of ours did it, because WE ARE HIS CHILDREN TOO!

Knowing what God did for us, it seems obvious that we have found favor with God. ALL WE HAVE TO DO IS BELIEVE THAT GOD GAVE US THIS GIFT! The "gate" to heaven will be open to anyone that accepts God's gift. (For gift acceptance details, refer to this lesson's rule!)

After receiving God's gift, and being armed with Grace and Faith, you will come to realize, that God wants us to always be in His good favor!

"What we are born with is God's gift to us." "What we do with it, is our gift to God."

--- anonymous (2)

Lesson 5..........Game of Life

THOUGHT: Some people digest life, and other people just get indigestion!

When God created earth and this physical world, He also made up a game called the Game of Life! Humans are the players that play in this game. Unfortunately, the Game of Life is not played on a fair and equal playing field. If you want any clarification of the game rules, ask God.

I will now give you the most general of general particulars, concerning the Game of Life. Please be aware that this is an incomplete description of the game. I am just trying to give you a quick overview, to make you picture the game, as you are reading along in this lesson. Are you ready? Here we go! Metaphorically speaking, when playing the Game of Life, a ball is what life throws at you. Life can throw curve balls, knuckle balls, fast balls, or even junk balls. And metaphorically speaking, you are a baseball bat that actually gets to hit the balls. You know, hit whatever life throws at you! A person can hit a single, get a strike, or hit a double. One can hit a foul, hit a triple, strike out, or hit a home run. You can apply this game to everything that happens to you in this life. For example: You just get done with a job interview, and you are offered a job; HOME RUN!

The earth is currently populated with about 7,000,000,000 players. Player development starts with genetics and then moves to the environment. Players grow socially, physically, and mentally.

Players can fall victim to random unknown forces, circumstances, and events. These occurrences might influence, disrupt, or even end a player's life. Other happenings can just as easily impact a player's life in positive ways!

I guess we could just say BAD happens to some: bad stuff, bad things, bad life! And GOOD happens to others: good stuff, good things, good Life! Life is not always one or the other. Most players have both good and bad things happen to them in their lives.

I can't remember, have I told you that the players who play in the Game of Life, do not play on a fair and equal playing field? Oh, I did? Oh, that's right, I did! Well then, great, just great. Just wanted to make sure that I did, that's all.

Let's take a look at some of the players who have already played the game.

Player (A) was born into a high society family. He grew up, and was smart, healthy, athletic, good looking, and rich. He led a good life, and he had a good life on earth. He died in his sleep at age 75.

Player (B) was a beautiful woman, full of life and energy. She was 21, and the whole world was in front of her. One night she was driving home from college when she fell asleep, and she lost control of her car. The car crashed into a tree, and her human body died.

Player (C) was born poor, and lived a very poor life. This player died, homeless and penniless.

Player (D) was just an average person. He had a wonderful family, a good job, and treated people nicely. One day he was driving home from work, when a drunk driver crossed over the center line, and crashed into his car. This average man survived, but spent the rest of his life in a wheel chair.

Player (E) was a female, who was smart, good looking, and athletic. She made a lot of friends throughout her entire life. She ended up having a great family and a rewarding career. During her life, she felt very blessed.

Player (F) was a child that was born with a genetic defect. The child spent most of his life in and out of hospitals. He died at age 12.

Player (G) was an entertainer of sort. He grew up and led a wild, chaotic, exotic life. At age 75 he married a 27- year-old swimsuit model. He was rich, and had a fun filled life. He died at age 95 of natural causes.

There is no guessing at this; life on earth is good for some, and bad for others. Life on earth is even great for some, yet it is terrible for others. In fact, LIFE ON EARTH IS MARVELOUS, WONDERFUL, AND FANTASTIC for a lot of people, but DEVASTING, PAINFUL, AND BRUTAL FOR OTHER PEOPLE.

If a rich man clings to God, because of all the blessings that he believes that God gives to him, and a poor man clings to God for hope and inspiration; upon their death, it is assumed that each of their souls would rise up and go through the gates of heaven for all eternity. If a rich man calls his life blessed, what does a poor man call his life?

Some people have everything they ever wanted in this physical life, while others do not. Why is that? It's my thought, that God does not shower us with blessings, nor does He shower us with problems. He gives one and all, opportunities and chances, along with Faith, Hope and Love. What?! More gifts?! He just keeps on giving and giving!

I believe that since the Holy Spirit lives in all of us, God loves everyone the same. Remember, God shares all of our feelings, and emotions; which include all of our pains, sufferings, joys, and triumphs.

God created this physical world for humans. Just for a minute, I would like you to think about yourself; you being a human, and all. I mean, really think about who you are physically, socially, and mentally. Think about all that you have been, all that you are, and all that you hope to be.

Now take the time to think about others in that same way. By doing this mental exercise, you will probably come to the same conclusion that I have: HUMANS ARE AN AMAZING SPECIES, AND GOD MADE US, SO HOW TRULY PERFECT HEAVENLY BEINGS MUST BE!

Now, I would like you to think about earth. Think about all the land masses, the waterways, different forms of life, the air we breathe, the water we drink, the food we consume, and all of earth's natural beauty. Then if that isn't enough for you to ponder, think about all the other things on earth life here has to offer you. After thinking about earth for a bit, you will probably realize that this planet is a wonderful place for humans to live. EARTH IS AN AMAZING PLANET, AND GOD MADE IT, SO HOW TRULY PERFECT HEAVEN MUST BE!

God allows the human race, and the planet that we live on, to be; for lack of a better word, HUMANLY. Humans can be: Good, bad, healthy, unhealthy, happy, depressed, lucky, unlucky, rich, poor, smart, not so smart, common, uncommon, neat, messy, loud, quiet, fun, dull, pretty, not so pretty, mean, nice, athletic, not athletic, short, tall, weak, strong, and the list could go on and on. HUMANS ARE WHAT THEY ARE, AND THE PLANET IS WHAT IT IS!

To keep everything in perspective, while we are here on earth, one only has to remember that our physical life is not a perfect life, and it is very much finite. Earth is a place where you have to accept the good with the bad, and so on, and so forth. SO BASICALLY, WE ARE AMAZING, YET, IMPERFECT BEINGS, LIVING IN AN AMAZING, YET, IMPERFECT WORLD!

Spiritual life in heaven is infinite, and heaven is pure, loving, beautiful, and perfect. God, in all His wisdom, made an imperfect world, because He wanted to make sure that all of His children would seek Him out. God made an imperfect world; isn't that a motivator to make us want to go to heaven?

Well, since we have already talked about the Game of Life, there should be nothing wrong with looking at the game in a competitive way. Bearing in mind all of the rules etc. found in the Bible, it makes no sense to any competitor, that there is only one chance to play in this game that we call life. From a competitor's stand point, it would even be okay if there was only one try at the Game of Life, if at the start of it, all the way to the end of it, all things were equal; health, riches, intellect, long life, etc. It would then be human against human, all competing to get into heaven, on an equal and level playing field.

To repeat myself: The Game of Life is not fair, and this everyone knows! Reflecting back to the day that I was born, which is not that easy you know, well anyway, I vaguely remember popping out and hearing a distant whistle. And then I am pretty sure that I heard God yell… "PLAY BALL!!!"

Don't do tobacco, alcohol, or other drugs, because they can sideline you from the Game of Life!

--- C.W.

If life was a cake...
You would have certain people thinking that life is a cakewalk.
Others would say that life is a piece of cake.
Some would get a bite of cake here and there.
Then there would be those, who only get the cake crumbs, and that is pretty crummy, no matter how you slice the cake!

--- C.W.

Is there a reason for us to be here? Heaven is perfect and infinite, and earth is imperfect and finite; I mean, why not just go directly to heaven?

--- C.W.

When is life ever simple? Short answer: It's not!

--- C.W.

"God has not promised us a quiet journey; only a safe arrival."

--- unknown (2)

Lesson 6... Life with the Holy Spirit

RULE: Keep the light within you, burning brightly!

It is common to refer to God as three persons: God the Father, God the Son (Jesus Christ), and God the Holy Spirit. The Holy Spirit plays an essential role in our physical life, and in our spiritual life. Just what role He plays, is kind of up to you, but, ultimately it is up to Him.

It is common to refer to a human being as one person, with one body, and one soul. A person's body is connected to this earthly life. A person's soul is connected to a person's body, and to the afterlife. The Holy Spirit is connected to a person's soul, and to heaven; which makes this the most awesome connection ever!

In lesson 3, I stated that we all should be happy and have joy in our hearts. When I wrote those words, they were a reflection of my thoughts, but I didn't spend much time trying to understand why I chose those words. But, now I get it! I totally get it! I understand now, why all of us should be happy and have joy in our hearts. I mean, why wouldn't we be happy and have joy in our hearts, if we knew that the Holy Spirit is within us! Knowing that our souls are filled with the Holy Spirit, should cause all of us to dance, celebrate, and rejoice! It's quite alright, if you do not like to express yourself in an outward manner; just go ahead and praise God inwardly. God will be happy either way.

Dang it, I just thought of a technicality, that might prevent some people from receiving the Holy Spirit. So, I have to ask, in lesson 4, did you accept God's gift? If yes, Wonderful! If no, go back to lesson 4, which really is only pages away, and I hope you choose with your heart to accept God's gift. Just open your heart and soul to God. He will literally and instantaneously come into your life, and by that time, your soul will have already been filled with the Holy Spirit, in one of God's mysterious ways.

Another way to refer to God is by saying that "God is Light." Let the Light of the Holy Spirit shine in you, and through you, for all to see. The Light inside of you, can be brilliantly bright, when your words, thoughts, prayers, actions, and good deeds make a strong connection with God. If later on, the connection, for whatever reason, gets weak and weaker, the Light within you, will become dim and dimmer. God, knowing that humans, are prone to sin, made arrangements to deal with this connectivity issue. God in all His Wisdom, allows our souls to get Holy Spirit re-fills, because He does not want any of His children to be in the dark. In fact, we can receive His Holy Spirit again, and again, and again. God has an infinite amount of Holy Spirit to give us, so He will keep on giving, if we keep on asking! At any time, or anywhere, you can ask God for a refill, or a recharge, to renew your relationship with Him.

Some people have fallen away from God who is Light, and live in shades of darkness. Satan, who is a fallen angel, lives in absolute darkness, where wickedness, sin and badness exist. Luckily for us, God is all about love and forgiveness! So, even those people who have engaged with the dark side, have the opportunity to return to God. All they have to do, is turn on the Light!

Since your body holds the Holy Spirit, be attentive to your body, with physical fitness, and good nutrition. And, don't forget about the Holy Spirit; it needs attention too! A human body lives, and a human body dies, but the Holy Spirit, and soul live on! Rumor has it, that the Holy Spirit, really enjoys church-time, Bible-time, and prayer-time. Let the Holy Spirit move you!

Bonus thought: While on earth, people from time to time, have Near Death Experiences. Some of them return from their experience, relating vivid accounts, of the reality of heaven. Spend time investigating this subject, and your faith in God will grow; which will make your soul glow.

Look at death from now on as a good thing, bad thing... Death: a really bad day for the body, but a really good day for the Holy Spirit, because the body turns to dust, and the Spirit gets to return to God!

--- C.W.

"The greatest evil that can befall a man is that he should come to think evil of himself."

--- Goethe (2)

"Let your light shine."

--- Matthew 5:16 (2)

"There is nothing the body suffers which the soul may not profit by."

--- George Meredith (2)

"Your body is the temple of the Holy Spirit, who lives in you, and was given to you by God."

--- 1Corinthians 6:19 (3)

You are never alone, because God is always with you!
--- C.W

ii

Lesson 7......... Life of the # 7

RULE: Think of the number 7, as being a very powerful number!

The number SEVEN shows up a lot in the Bible. Perhaps God uses that specific number, to get us to REMEMBER HIM!

When you are reading the Bible, and you come across the number 7, the first thing that should pop into your head is God! It stands to reason, that if you come across the number 7, even when you are not reading the Bible, God will still pop into your head for a second or two; and that could be exactly what God had in mind.

Numbers have always been, and are still very much, an important part of our life. It only makes sense that God would want to have a presence in our number system, as well as in our words.

The # 7, in and of itself, has no power, because it is only a number. The power comes when you see the number 7, and you instantly think of God.

As the number 7 is associated with God, the number 6 is associated with Satan.

Let's have some number fun, with the number 7... 7 times.

1.) Mathematically speaking, 7 is a stronger number than 6, because the number 7 is a prime number!

2.) In mathematical terms, the number 7 has power over the number 6, since the number 7 is a bigger number.

3.) 7 minus 6 = 1, and there is only one God.

4.) 7 plus 6 = 13, and the number (13) can represent the conflict between good and evil.

5.) 7 rhymes with heaven!

6.) There are 7 things expressed in the Lord's Prayer.

7.) A rainbow has 7 visible colors.

7 QUOTES

"The shortest and surest way to live with honor in the world is to be, in reality, what we appear to be."

--- Socrates (2)

"Things turn out best for those who make the best of the way things turn out."

--- Art Linkletter (2)

"Courage means being afraid to do something, but still doing it."

--- Knute Rockne (2)

"Every moment of your life, including this one, is a fresh start."

--- unknown (2)

"Whatever one believes to be true, either is true or becomes true in one's mind."

--- John C. Lilly (2)

"The universe is change; our life is what our thoughts make it."

--- Marcus Aurelius Antoninus (2)

"I have prepared for death all my life, by the way I lived."

--- Socrates (2)

Lesson 8.............Prayer Life

RULE: Spend at least 1 minute a day praying to God, praising God, thanking God, or just talking to God.

A lot of people have the whole prayer thing customized, and individualized to the point that their prayers are more like shopping lists of individual wants and needs.

Instead of praying to God the way we want to, let us pray to God the way He would like us to pray to Him. Let us put God before ourselves! Do you remember when He put us before Himself?

BY WAY OF THE LORD'S PRAYER, JESUS SHOWED ALL OF US HOW TO PRAY!

God already knows what your individual wants and needs are. You do not need to pray for what God already knows. And God doesn't just want to hear from us when we are up to bat and the bases are loaded, and all He can hear is: "Please God, please God, please let me hit this ball over the fence; please, please, please!" Although spontaneous conversations with God are well and good, one should take the time to really THINK ABOUT GOD, THANK GOD, and PRAISE GOD.

When the things people pray for happen, do you think it is the power of prayer, a flip of a coin, a chance happening, or a coincidence? Let me give you a hypothetical example that in real life has undoubtedly happened. Variations of this example, with different circumstances, happen a lot in this world!

Two Christian families both had a sick family member in the hospital. Both were children, who were expected to die. The two children shared the same hospital room and had the same medical problem. Family members of each child gathered in the same room each day, being separated by only a curtain. One hospital bed on one side of the curtain, and one hospital bed on the other side of the curtain. One day all of the family members for both kids were in the room, standing in their respective areas. Each family began to pray that their loved one's sickness would pass and that their son, daughter, brother, sister, grand-daughter, grand-son, be allowed to live. After a day or two had passed since the two prayer meetings, medical personnel told one set of parents, that their child was going to be okay. The parents who received the good news along with other relatives walked into the above hospital room, and paraded around showing signs of joy, happiness, and relief. One of the family members, for whatever reason, pulled away the curtain that was still separating the two sides of the hospital room. When the curtain was pulled back it revealed that no one was on the other side of the room. The second bed, where the other child had been, was still there, but the child was conspicuously missing. During the night, this child had died.

After people pray, they end up perceiving that their prayers, were either answered or unanswered. Both answered and unanswered prayers may be a match with God's plan. But, the truth is, that none of us actually know what God's plan is! Regardless of this, it is very important for us to pray, and pray, and pray, with the knowledge, that God hears all of our prayers. While you are doing all that praying, keep in mind that OUR GOD, is an all-powerful God, that can exercise His right, to bless anyone, or any situation, at any time.

Prayers come in many forms, such as, asking prayers, thanking prayers, and praising prayers. Use the power of prayer, to reach out to God, and maybe, possibly influence Him. You never know, a miracle just may happen!

It's awesome, that miracles do happen, which neither science nor man can explain. May your eyes be open to miracles, both big and small. Don't discount a meaningful coincidence, it may indeed qualify as a miracle!

The Bible contains the Lord's Prayer, which shows all of us, how to pray to our one God. This is a common version of the Lord's Prayer. JESUS ACTUALLY SPOKE THESE WORDS:

"Our Father, who art in heaven,

Hallowed be thy name.

Thy Kingdom come,

Thy will be done, on earth as it is in heaven.

Give us this day our daily bread.

And forgive us our trespasses, as we forgive those who trespass against us.

And lead us not into temptation, but deliver us from Evil."

The "Give us this day our daily bread" line, definitely gives us all a big hint, that this prayer should be said every day. Keep in mind this is not an individual grocery list type prayer. When you say the Lord's Prayer, you are saying words like (WE) and (US). This prayer has people praising God, forgiving each other, and praying for one another. The power of one prayer.................. AWESOME!

A good way to make this prayer meaningful to you, and more personal between you and God, is to begin the Lord's Prayer by making the sign of the cross. When making the sign of the cross you can focus on God the Father, God the Son, and God the Holy Spirit. By doing this, you will make God's words live in your mind, in your heart, and in your soul.

The following can be done silently, or out loud; reader's choice!

Move one hand up, and lightly touch your finger tips to your forehead and say: "God the Father, let me be mindful of you."

The fingertips of the same hand are now placed over your heart, and are actually touching your chest, while saying: "God the Son, let me think about your human heart beating, while you were dying on the cross for me."

The same hand now moves to one shoulder, and then to the other shoulder when you say: "God the Holy Spirit, let me be aware that you are a part of me."

After this salutation, continue your prayer time with God, by saying the Lord's Prayer.

The following is "my" interpretation of the Lord's Prayer. I am not replacing God's words, with my words. I am simply using my words, in an attempt, to understand His words. However you may interpret the Lord's Prayer, just make His words, and your words meaningful to you!

1.) Our God in heaven,

2.) We (the human race) honor You, and Your name.

3.) At any time, let Your Heavenly Kingdom come upon us (the human race); we welcome You.

4.) Let Your will be done on earth as it is in heaven. Let us (the human race) accept Your plans, before our own plans.

5.) Please give us (the human race) what we (the human race) need this day.

6.) Forgive us (the human race) for our sins, as we (the human race) forgive those who commit sins against us (the human race).

7.) Do not let us (the human race) stray from Your will, and keep us (the human race) from thinking bad thoughts, and doing bad things. Protect us (the human race) from all that is evil.

I know that the average person is kept busy, day after day, with, you guessed it; day to day things. Not that I timed it or anything, but the Lord's Prayer can be respectfully, and meaningfully delivered to God in about one minute. Even on your busiest day, take one minute to focus on God, and on the rest of God's children, which of course, includes you.

You are probably wondering if God would be okay with a relationship that only lasts sixty seconds a day? Yes!! ....of course He would.

"Timing has a lot to do with the outcome of the rain dance."

--- unknown author (2)

"Prayer never seems to work for me on the golf course. I think it has something to do with my being a terrible putter."

--- Rev. Billy Graham (2)

When talking about the American Civil War, Abraham Lincoln once said: "We, on our side are praying for victory, because we believe we are right; but those on the other side pray to Him too, for victory, believing they are right. What must He think of us?"

--- (2)

Lesson 9......Rainbow of Life

RULE: Enjoy this life, and play nicely with others!

Let's just say that at one-time God was not pleased with all the violence, and probably some other things that He saw in the world, so He kind of let it rain and rain………and rain…………and rain, until it rained so much that it flooded the earth.

"Then God told Noah and his sons, I am making a covenant with you and your descendants." "I solemnly promise never to send another flood to kill all living creatures and destroy the earth." "I am giving you a sign as evidence of my eternal covenant with you and all living creatures." "I have placed my rainbow in the clouds." "It is the sign of my permanent promise to you and to all earth." "When I send clouds over the earth the rainbow will be seen in the clouds, and I will remember my covenant with you and with everything that lives." "Never again will there be a flood that will destroy all life." "When I see the rainbow in the clouds, I will remember the eternal covenant between God and every living creature on earth." "Then God said to Noah," "Yes, this is the sign of my covenant with all the creatures of the earth." ------- Genesis 8 (3)

The rainbow can be seen all over the world! I'm pretty sure everyone has seen a rainbow, but a rainbow is just a rainbow, unless you know exactly what a rainbow is. Yes, there is the scientific definition of course, but getting past all of the scientific jargon, a rainbow is a visual reminder of a promise that God made to all of us. The promise that God made, is a PROMISE OF LIFE! Now that you know about the promise, I hope when you look at a rainbow from now on, you will keep that in mind.

Since the promise was for the entire human race, it makes perfect sense that God would give us a rainbow to symbolize all the many colors that make up the human race. And I bet you already know how many colors are in a rainbow; am I right? Hint: It rhymes with Heaven.

When you are looking up at the next rainbow that you see, and you are thinking about God, these are the 7 shades of colors that you might see: red, orange, yellow, green, blue, indigo, and violet.

Did you notice, that I did not mention anything about Leprechauns or about that elusive pot of gold at the end of a rainbow? And all for good reasons, because finding a pot of gold at the end of a rainbow may not be in your future, but finding treasure in heaven may well be within your reach!

"The greatest joy one can have is doing something for someone else, without any thought of getting something in return."

--- John Wooden (2)

"I shall pass through the world but once. Any good therefore that I can show to another human being, let me do it now."

--- Mahatma Gandhi (2)

"You can never do a kindness too soon, because you never know how soon it will be too late."

--- Ralph Waldo Emerson (2)

"The smallest good deed is better than the best intention."

--- unknown (2)

"I always seek the good that is in people and leave the bad to Him who made mankind and knows how to round off the corners."

--- Goethe (2)

Lesson 10.... Purpose of Life

THOUGHT: The purpose of life; is living life.

God gave all of us a purpose way back when! "Male and Female He created them." "God blessed them and told them," "Multiply and fill the Earth... " ------ - Genesis 1 (3)

When you are married, and you don't have any kids, you can say my purpose in life, but when you have kids, it is mandated somewhere, that MY gets changed to OUR. My wife was my purpose in life, but when our kids showed up on the scene, they became OUR purpose in life. To clarify things a little bit more, what I should have said was that my wife is still MY purpose in life, but our kids are OUR purpose in life. It is the same purpose, but only much bigger.

My family story began, when I married the love of my life. At that time, my purpose in life was pretty simple; all I wanted to do, was to be a great husband to my wife. We wanted kids someday, but we first wanted to make sure that we had a solid relationship before we had them. One of the things we learned early on, is that a simple touch went a long way in making both of us feel good about each other, and about our relationship.

On any given day, my wife and I hold hands. Sometimes we give each other spontaneous quick little kisses and hugs. At times, we just have a hand, arm, or leg touching each other while we are sitting on the couch, or when we are sleeping in bed. It's not like we play twister on the couch and in bed or anything, but we just end up touching each other a lot. And yes, all of the other ways that we touch each other are just as important as the intimate touching, because any touch sends the message of trust and love, and those two words should be a part of any marriage.

Our relationship grew, our love grew, and then a baby life, in my wife, grew, and grew, and grew... and then poof! Our first child was born... and then we yelled: "WE ARE PARENTS... YES!!!!" After the initial celebration, I looked at my wife, and my wife looked at me, and then we looked at our baby in her arms, and we both screamed: "WE ARE PARENTS?!!"

My purpose in life went from simple, to not so simple. I started to think about the fact that my wife and I were now responsible for another LIFE! Later on, not that same day or anything, we had our second child, and MY purpose in life, oops; I mean OUR purpose in life, got even BIGGER!

I don't care how many times, or how many ways, that you tell a new couple about how their lives will change when they have kids; they will not fully comprehend any of it, until after their first baby is born. And when that happens, they will know right away that a parent's, purposeful, purpose is based on LOVE. Later on, it will become apparent to them, that a parent's purpose, lasts a life-time. As the family tree grows, so does their purpose.

There are additional purposes in life besides marriage and family. I mean, one does not have to be married, or have a family, to have purpose.

The purpose IN life, OF life, or TO life, can be anything you love to do, and have a passion for doing; as long as you are willing to share whatever it is you like to do with God. It can be things like golfing, cooking, bird watching, hiking, reading, fishing, hunting, going to work, having a hobby, playing or watching sports, anything and everything can be purposeful. Hey, what do you know, I just thought of two more purposes. It would be remiss of me, not to add them to the list; since they are such noble purposes. The first one is to help others, and the second one is to spread the awesome news about Jesus Christ. The thing to remember, is that the purpose of this life, is to have purpose in this life, or in most cases, purposes!

If you keep an eye to heaven when you are living this life, you will add purpose to your life; which, as it turns out, is the single most important purpose of them all! This purpose is to live life, with the life goal of being in the next life; which is... an eternal life with God!

"A hug is a great gift. One size fits all and it's easy to exchange."
--- unknown (2)

"To be trusted is a greater compliment than to be loved."
--- George MacDonald (2)

"Make yourself necessary to somebody."
--- Ralph Waldo Emerson (2)

Lesson 11....... Words of Life

RULE: Keep God's words alive!

The Bible was put together by collecting way more, than A LOT, of probably written documents, letters, stories, books, and other miscellaneous writings. The Bible was actually put together by humans. Bravo for the human race; we actually did a good thing. But humans, through no fault of their own are, well, human! When we think back to when people were working on the Bible for a very, very, very... long time, it is pretty darn easy for any of us to assume that some of the material may have been left out for one reason or another. During the process of making the Bible words had to be interpreted, translated, and rewritten. Words could have also been intentionally deleted, or added, to existing texts. After the original Bible was made the words again had to be interpreted, translated, and re-written into different languages. I am not trying to imply that the Bible was put together incorrectly in any way. What I'm trying to convey is that God did not write the Bible; He inspired others to write the Bible.

What did I just say? I said: THE BIBLE WAS WRITTEN BY MAN; INSPIRED BY GOD.

Though there were countless verbal and written testimonies, scrolls, papers, stories, documents, pictures, books, and other writings present when the pages to the Bible were compiled, not all of it was used; which means there is probably still enough left-over material somewhere, that could still be used to make a Bible 2. Obviously, no one was thinking of a Hollywood movie deal when this thing was being planned out; I guess they had more Godly interests in mind.

Biblical scholars, now and in the past, with faith at their sides, hold the Bible up, and announce the Bible to be the work of God! The Bible has withstood the test of time, and if anything, the words in the Bible are growing more and more powerful each day. I encourage one and all to read the Bible with an open mind, an open heart, and with the awareness that the Holy Spirit is a part of you.

The Bible holds the living words of God, such as the Lord's Prayer and the Ten Commandments. Other words in the Bible show us how much God loves all of us. As long as people keep reading the Bible, talking about the Bible, interpreting the Bible, either correctly or incorrectly, discussing topics in the Bible or even debating things that are in the Bible, God's words will stay alive. As long as these things happen God will not be forgotten, and God will be pleased.

If we were to mention one of those debated topics, I guess we could talk about baptism. You know; the whole wash away your sins ritual. To wash, or not to wash? That is the question. Well, we know that Jesus was baptized, so that bit of information has to be pretty good for the people on the one side of the topic. People on the other side, say that baptism is not a mandatory thing for entering heaven. Mandatory, or non-mandatory? That is the new question. Well, since there is nothing wrong with doing a little extra credit when trying to get into heaven, I think a better question to ask is: When and where can I wash?!! And just so everyone is in the loop regarding this subject, baptism in general, is when water is symbolically used to wash away your sins; as opposed to you jumping in a tub with a bar of soap!

God made it very clear that He wanted us to obey all of His commandments. If it was important enough for Him to say the words, and have them put in the Bible, then I know they are important enough for me to put them in my book.

GOD SPOKE THESE WORDS:

1.) "Do not worship any other God besides Me." My interpretation - Love God.

2.) "Do not make idols of any kind." My interpretation - Do not bow down or worship anything, or anybody, except God.

3.) "Do not misuse the name of the Lord your God." My interpretation - Only say God's name in respectful ways.

4.) "Remember to observe the Sabbath day by keeping it holy." My interpretation – Church for some, rest for others, but honoring God, should be for everyone. You can honor God daily by saying the Lord's Prayer.

5.) "Honor your father and mother." My interpretation - Always be respectful of your parents.

6.) "Do not murder." My interpretation - Do not murder; which includes the taking of your own life.

7.) "Do not commit adultery." My interpretation - Do not "cheat" on your spouse, or "cheat" with another person's spouse.

8.) "Do not steal." My interpretation - Do not take things that don't belong to you.

9.) "Do not testify falsely against your neighbor." My interpretation - Do not lie.

10.) "Do not covet your neighbor's house." My interpretation - Do not be jealous of anything that someone else might have.

Did you know if you spend about 15 minutes a day reading the Bible, you could finish reading the Bible in the same amount of time that it takes the earth to make one lap around the sun? Just for your information, it takes approximately 365 days for the earth to circle the sun one time. Well, if you are not interested in racing the earth around the sun, simply put your Bible out somewhere in your house, and read the Bible whenever you want, for as long as you want. God is probably okay if you just look at the cover of the Bible when you are coming and going, because when you look at the cover, you think about God, and that works for Him! God just doesn't want to be forgotten.

The Bible has been around for generations, and generations, and generations, and generations, but in the Bible ------- Matthew 4(3) it says: "The Kingdom of Heaven is near.".... define NEAR!... When trying to interpret the word NEAR I guess it could still mean time, but wonder if it was talking about distance? I wonder if it means heaven is close to us right now?

--- C.W.

"Many people are bothered by those passages in the scripture which they cannot understand; but as for me, I always noticed that the passages in scripture which trouble me the most are those I do understand."

--- Mark Twain (2)

Lesson 12 The Life of a Super Hero

RULE: Just say NO!

The Super Power of saying NO! It's not the coolest type of power as far as all the powers that are given out in the Super Hero community; nevertheless, it's a great power to have!

The power to say NO, can keep the NO Super Hero physically and mentally strong. This power is so great, that by using it, a NO Super Hero can even CONTROL a situation that could be harmful to them physically, mentally, and socially. Other Super Heroes have never been given a power like this; this power is unique only to humans. Can you name a Super Hero that has this power?... I can name one:_____ (You!)

This power can be used in many situations. When asked to use tobacco products, or alcohol you have the power to say NO. When asked to have sex when you really don't want to, you have the power to say NO. Before doing any unlawful acts, you have the power to say NO. When asked to smoke marijuana, or do other drugs, you have the power to say NO. When you are thinking about cheating at something, you have the power to tell yourself NO. Before telling a lie, you have the power to tell yourself NO. The list goes on and on. This power can be used for virtually everything that comes across your path in this life.

All Super Heroes have senses that alert them to when danger is close by, or even when it is somewhere out in the distance. The important thing is to not work against your Super Power.

When your senses pick up danger, and they warn you mentally that this, that, or the other thing is not going to be good for you, in one way or the other, then don't question your Super Power; act on it by saying NO! Having this Super Power comes with great responsibility when trying to protect yourself.

At times, you might be face to face with danger and need an instant NO. Other times you will be able to say NO ahead of time, so you don't put yourself in a bad situation. Just believe in your Super Hero Power and always use it.

Oh, one more cool thing, all NO Super Heroes can put their NO response on automatic pilot. This protects them if something in life jumps up, and surprises them so much, that their Super Hero senses are not able to give them a clear alert signal. When this happens, the automatic pilot drops a NO bomb instantly. By having a built in automatic "NO" response, a Super Hero is protected immediately; which will give any Super Hero time enough to evaluate everything. If, after a few seconds, minutes, hours, or days, it is found that the surprise was a good thing, as opposed to being a bad thing, then the Super Hero can go ahead and throw away the NO, and say yes. Please do not worry about wasting a NO here or there; you have an unlimited supply of them, because, after all, you are a Super Hero.

If you fail to use this Super Power in a given situation, it could lead to negative consequences for you, and your life; and that would not be good for any Super Hero.

If you ever give up your Super Hero Power, and say yes to alcohol, tobacco, and other drugs; these things can have power over you. At one point, you will want to say NO, but your mind, and your body will work against you.

ADDICTION IS REAL! HEALTH RISKS ARE REAL! SELF IMPOSED UGLINESS!!

It's hard to "live life" when you are living each day for a drug. MAY YOUR SUPER POWER ALWAYS BE WITH YOU!!!!

Three daily reminders: Have the courage to say NO! Have the courage to face the truth. Have the courage to do the right thing, because it is right."

--- W. Clement Stone (2)

Lesson 13......Life's Choices

RULE: Life is not to be understood, but lived.

One of the best ways to live your earthly life is to always try to do the right thing. I mean really, after all, wouldn't that be the right thing to do?

It is true that anything and everything can happen to us at any time; some of it good, some of it bad, some of it really good, and some of it really bad, but that's life! One can spend their entire life trying to understand life. It just may be that LIFE IS NOT TO BE UNDERSTOOD, BUT LIVED, and to live it the best way we can. One does not have to understand this life to live this life!

God has given humans free will, so living life means making choices, and the choices we make will ultimately define the person that we are, or the person that we will become. With that being said, God asks all of us to follow His will on earth as we would in heaven. He gives us free will, yet He wants us to use our free will to follow His will, if we are willing to do that. I guess I will leave that one up to you, because after all, you do have a free will!

In any given evil situation in which we find ourselves, we should walk away from it, and try to follow in the footsteps of Jesus. Since we are humans, it is possible for us to walk away from any situation, but not so possible to walk in Jesus' footsteps. However, if you do come up against any evil encounters, and at the end of them you know that you did the right thing or gave the right response, or you knew that you were right, in the eyes of God; then I'm quite positive you will find your own path to heaven.

God just wants us to enjoy this earthly life as much as possible, while still maintaining a God approved life style. As humans, let us try our best, and let God take care of the rest.

To recap what has already been said: God in His amazing wisdom allows all humans to be unique in their own individual ways. He does this by giving us free choice in everything we do; good luck with that!

"There is a choice you have to make in everything you do. And you must always keep in mind that the choice you make, makes you."

--- anonymous (2)

"Choose your friends carefully. If you hang with dogs you'll end up with fleas."

--- unknown (2)

"Take pride in yourself. Be your own person. Don't do things because everyone else does them. Don't be a part of the crowd. Dare to be different. Never be afraid to stand up for what you believe to be right, even when it means standing alone."

--- Jack Lambert (2)

"Never undertake anything that you would not have the courage to ask the blessing of heaven."

--- Georg Christian Lichtenberg (2)

Lesson 14...... Life with Faith

RULE: Stay strong, and put God first!

Faith verses knowledge: It's apparent, that while on earth, God is only going to allow us to have a little bit of knowledge; so, faith is what we cling to. It stands to reason that all beings in heaven can let go of their faith, and just live KNOWINGLY, in God's Kingdom. KNOWINGLY; wouldn't that be something?

Even though faith is a workable system in a religious setting, I still think that it would be cool if God would just open up the sky, present Himself to us, and tell us exactly how to live the kind of life that He wants us to live.

If God were to open up the sky and show Himself to us, the meeting would probably go something like this: We would see our God above the clouds. Some human would yell: "Give us direction;" "Give us the rules to live the kind of life that you want us to live." God would reply by saying: "I ALREADY DID!!" "Do the TEN COMMANDMENTS ring any bells?!" Then the sky would return to normal.

If that meeting did take place, and God did not verbally go over the details of living a good life, the way I figure it, it still would have been a win - win situation. We have the Bible and the 10 Commandments, like we have always had. And the face to face meeting with God, would have increased everyone's faith in God exponentially!

Well, as of yet, that face to face meeting has not taken place. So, if you want to increase your faith in God, spend some time concentrating on God, and on the relationship, that you have with Him. Reading the Bible, and praying also help in the process of strengthening your faith, but it is the mental strength that will make your faith strong. You know the kind of strength I'm referring to; the kind when you're able to FOCUS ON GOD FIRST, AND THIS EARTHLY LIFE SECOND!

As mentioned in lesson 6, humans are prone to sin, but it is possible that a person's faith, with a little help from the Holy Spirit, can be developed to the point that a person can move mountains! Although it is possible, it is not very probable, because, well, after all, we are human! (See Matthew 17:20)

Extra Bonus Thought: When comparing eternal life, to our lives now, we come to realize that we are here on earth, for only a second or two; which, if you think about it, actually gives us plenty of time to start a trusting relationship with our God. Trust happens, when we mentally give everything in our lives to God, and don't worry, we will get it all back in heaven; and then some!

"The spirit and faith that we possess inside each of us is what really matters."

--- Socrates (2)

"I do not want merely to possess faith; I want a faith that possesses me."

--- Charles Kingsley (2)

"Faith dares the soul to go further than we can see."

--- William Clark (2)

"Security is not the absence of danger; it is the presence of God."

--- unknown (2)

"The Lord is my strength, of whom should I be afraid?"

--- Psalm 27:1 (2)

"The greatness of our fear shows the littleness of our faith."

--- anonymous (2)

Lesson 15.......Life In...Worry Out

RULE: Pull God in, and push worry and control issues out!

Should we worry about all of the things that we can't control, or try to control all of the things that we worry about?

People should not worry about what they don't have control over, because they are not going to be able to live life if they are too busy worrying about it. It could be stated, that people do not have control over anything, and God has control over everything!

I guess, in some ways, human beings do have a little control over what they eat and drink, think, say and do. We shuffle these things into the self-control category.

IN QUESTIONABLE MATTERS, THE HIGHEST LEVEL OF SELF-CONTROL OCCURS WHEN A PERSON THINKS AND THEN LISTENS TO THE HOLY SPIRIT, BEFORE SAYING OR DOING ANYTHING.

What do we know so far? We know that on a personal level we have hardly any control over our lives. And guess what? We can't control other people, or what happens to them either! We have no control regarding what happens to us, or around us. Basically, we have gone from having no control, to having some control, and now we are back to having no control; is that about right?

Let's be mindful of the fact that the mind can work for you, as well as work against you. Some worry-wart type thoughts can even consume you. They eat at you, and eat at you, until you are mentally spent, and exhausted. When you think about it, some thoughts can be so thoughtless! I am not a psychologist; however, I bet if you were to make an appointment to see one, the psychologist would tell you pretty much the same things, that I just told you. On a Christian level, if you are focusing on God, I mean really focusing your thoughts on God, you can eliminate useless worrying. Focusing on God can be done anywhere, and everywhere, without an appointment!

Control issues and worry issues should no longer be your issues. If you are a person that tends to worry, and attempts to control things, then I guess, you should be upset that it is pointless and meaningless to worry about anything, because generally speaking, you don't have control over anything; you only have control over nothing. Hey, wait a second! Wait a darn second here. What did I just say? Did I just say something about nothing? I think, I said something about actually having control over something, which is nothing. Oh! Wow! The mud has been wiped away, and things are now crystal clear. It is a glorious day for all worriers and controllers, because now it has been brought out in the open. There is finally something that worriers can worry about, and have control over, and that something is NOTHING!!!

If you are a worrier, you now have a choice! You can either worry about anything, or you can worry about nothing. For those of you, who choose to worry about nothing, refer to the framed pictures at the beginning of this lesson. There, inside of the frames, you will actually get to see what nothing looks like!

It is hoped that worriers will not add extra worry to their day, by worrying about how silly it is to worry about nothing. Because when you think about it, worrying about anything is just as silly! Still, if you like a busy day, worrying will surely keep you occupied. If you decide that you want to free up your time, to live the way that God wants you to live life, just throw all of your "ANYTHINGS" and "NOTHINGS" to God.

"Can all your worries add a single moment to your life? Of course not."

--- Mathew 6:27(3)

"Worry is a futile thing, it's somewhat like a rocking chair; although it keeps you occupied, it doesn't get you anywhere."

--- anonymous (2)

"Good morning! This is God. I will be handling all of your problems today, and I will not need your help. Just stay close to Me and enjoy your day."

--- unknown

Lesson 16......... Church Life

RULE: Love and respect your neighbors.

At one time, all humans spoke the same language. "The Lord confused the people by giving them many languages thus scattering them across the earth." ------- Genesis 11(3)

I'm just ball parking it here; but I'm guessing that God did not want us all to be the same. God wanted people to have different languages, and different cultures. And guess what? That's exactly what He got.

When God populated the world, and separated the human race, it is only logical that different cultures would grow to have different religions. He wanted dissimilar religions reaching out to Him and praising His name in divergent ways!

Well, this much we know: In the world, there are numerous people, different cultures, different languages, and different religions.

There are 7 billion people spread out all over the world in North America, Asia, Africa, Europe, South America, and other places.

The languages spoken are: Chinese, English, Spanish, Hindi, Arabic, Russian, Bengali, Portuguese, Japanese, German, French, and others.

The religions all over the world are: Christianity, Islam, Hinduism, Judaism, Buddhism, and others.

We are all God's children, so let us all be good neighbors and love each other! The good neighbor policy states that we should respect each other's culture, religion, and language. And since we all live in the same neighborhood called earth, it would be a very good thing if we didn't judge each other! That way we can be respectfully free, to shout out, and praise God, in the way that works for each one of us!

This would probably be a good time, for me to tell you, that I am a lot more unknowledgeable, than I am knowledgeable, about all of the different religions.

I am hopeful that all religions, give people a base, from which to reach our one God. It is assumed, that all religions allow for some separation of beliefs, ideas, and doctrines. A person in any given religion can even have an individual, personal belief system. If a religion can lead to God, then I guess that all of the many ways of worshiping Him, within a given religion, can lead to God too!

In my opinion, for a religion to meet the needs of the human race, it needs to be able to reach out to God, connect with God and provide a pathway to God.

Can all religions in one way or another lead to our one God?...... Maybe?........ Maybe not? ....CHOOSE WISELY!

Since you are reading my book, I feel like I should share something with you. I WANT YOU TO BE IN THE KNOW....... about something that I know. And I know, what I know, because what I am about to tell you, comes from my heart, my mind and my soul. Here is what I know:

"Christianity reaches out to God, connects with God and provides a pathway to God; HALLELUJAH!!!!!!!"

Now that you know, what I know, you know it is still up to you, right? A religion can only take you so far in your journey, it will be up to you, to actually reach God.

Let's just say that Christianity, or the Christian religion is the right religion for you. And if being active in this religion, is important to you, then you will need to decide on how, and where to worship God. The cool thing for Christians right now, is that there are a number churches, all honoring God in their own way.

A church is a very special place, because of what it represents. It represents a "House of God." If someone asked me what my definition of church would be, I would simply say: COMMUNITY, SOCIAL INTERACTION, DOCTRINE, AND A HOUSE IN WHICH TO PRAISE GOD.

God likes that whole love thy neighbor thing, and that love and neighbor thing fits a church like a glove. A church is a great place to meet your neighbors. A neighbor is not just the person who lives next door to you. A neighbor, in the biblical sense of the word, means the human race; so, good luck planning a dinner party for all of your neighbors!

The good thing about there being so many churches, is that you can pick the right church for you. You will want to feel comfortable with the church leaders, the church doctrine, and the people who attend the church. When this happens, it will be a match made in heaven, so to speak.

Go ahead and become a member of any church in which you would like to get involved. Churches give us memberships, that can facilitate our relationship with God. God gives us LIFE and SALVATION. HAVE A MEMBERSHIP IN A CHURCH, AND FAITH IN GOD!

"If I were ever prosecuted for my religion, I truly hope there would be enough evidence to convict me."

--- John Wooden (2)

"Not always right in all men's eyes, but faithful to the light within."

--- Oliver Wendell Holmes (2)

"To believe in something and not live it, is dishonest."

--- Ghandi (2)

"I am just a common man that is true to his beliefs."
                                        --- John Wooden (2)

We are the same in really only one way; we are all humans. We are different in so many ways, because we are human. Let us celebrate the fact that we are all human beings, and respect each of our many differences.
                                        --- C.W.

"I looked for God in all the temples, mosques, and churches, and found Him in my heart."   ---unknown

STONEHENGE

Lesson 17......... Societal Life

RULE: View all current societies as changing in an ultra-slow, continual, and positive progression. That way you can accept the world's present societies the way they are, as opposed to the way you want them to be.

I'm sure all over the world there are people in each given society saying things like: "Our society is really messed up." People who say things like that, obviously, do not adhere to the rule in this training lesson.

To continue the training, we will just go ahead and pick on the United States. It appears that some people have been complaining about various problems in this society. Here is a list of things that some of the American people are, shall we say, commenting negatively on: education, healthcare, unemployment, and the criminal justice system.

The above list is a bit overwhelming, but to be fair to the United States, the lists for the other societies in this world are just as long. To have people gain a new perspective on things, so they can view their own society, and/or all of the societies in the world in a positive way, we only have to give them a glimpse of the past; then have them participate in a small training exercise.

Two of the first ancient civilizations were Mesopotamia, and Ancient Egypt. Those two ancient societies lasted well over 2,000 years. After the above two societies ended, there were others to take their place. From the first societies, to the present-day societies, there have been thousands of years of ultra-slow, continual, and positive progression. The U.S.A. came about in 1776 AD and this book came about in 2017 AD. There are only 241 years that separate 1776 from 2017; which means, this country has a long way to go, and grow, before it reaches the 1000 year mark!

Now that we have had a brief look at the past, the training exercise can begin. It starts when participants mentally take a trip backwards through time and envision themselves, as being non-royals, living in one of the ancient civilizations. The trainees have an up close, mental awakening when they look at the politics, power, culture, religion, science, technology, and the people that made up the first societies.

After the participants come back from the short trip, they are asked only one question: "Do you want to live in your present society, or would you rather go back in time, if it was possible, which it is not, and live in one of the first societies?"

The responses have always been pretty much the same. They say things like: "No matter how messed up our present-day society is, we will take here and now, instead of then and there!"

During the retrospective training session, the trainees were never told how any of the modern day societal problems could be fixed. But maybe, just maybe, the trainees will now, at least, be able to put on rose colored, new perspective eye glasses, and see the problems in our society as being only WORKS IN PROGRESS!

Societies have only been around for approximately 5,000 years. In comparison to the age of the earth, societies have only existed for a very short period of time. You can say that again!! In comparison to the age of the earth, societies have only existed for a very short period of time; which of course, leaves room for lots of improvements!

From time to time it is good to look back into the past, because the past is our beginning, and without a past, there is no beginning, and that would not be good for any of us. The past should not be forgotten, or dismissed. The ability to write, and document history was very much present in Ancient Egypt and Mesopotamia. Learned things were, and continue to be, passed on from one generation to the next. We should respect all those who have come before us, because they have made our world a better place to live.

There have been numerous historical events recorded in one way or another. One particular event deeply impacted the world! That event was the life and death of Jesus Christ, Our Lord and Savior.

Wow! Christ's life impacted the world so much that even the calendar system was adapted to separate old world history, BC, with new world history, AD, and the birth of Jesus was the dividing line.

BC stands for "Before Christ," and AD stands for "Anno Domini; which means in the year of the Lord." The intent to divide the periods was there, but the dividing line was just a tad off, because later it was learned that Jesus was born around "6 to 4 BC," and died around "33 AD." Nevertheless, God's mark; "AD" was left on the world's calendar for everyone to see. Question: "What year was this book published?" Answer: 2017 "AD." There He goes again; not wanting to be forgotten! (1)

The United States of America is so new, that it is still working out all of the kinks... obviously!

--- C.W.

"Individual commitment to a group effort – that is what makes a team work, a company work, a society work, and civilization work."

--- Vince Lombardi (2)

"Most things that were once believed impossible are now common place."

--- unknown (2)

"You must be the change that you wish to see in the world."

--- Ghandi (2)

Society punishes people when they break criminal laws... it's called jail. We punish ourselves regarding moral laws... it's called guilt.

--- C.W.

Human ingenuity; reach God any way that you can!

--- C.W.

Lesson 18........ Life on the Big Screen

RULE: What happens on the big screen should stay on the big screen. (Please apply this rule to questionable shows).

Hollywood has desensitized the human race regarding violence, sex, drugs, alcohol, cigarettes, cigars, swearing, crimes and saying God's name in disrespectful ways. The amount of influence that a given show has on its viewers is tremendous. When kids and adults see actors being violent, having sex, doing drugs, drinking alcohol, smoking, swearing, committing crimes, and saying God's name in disrespectful ways, it is bound to influence them in negative ways.

Watching shows produced by Hollywood, or other sources, is a free choice thing. If you find yourself watching a show, that your great, great, grandmother would probably not approve of, then follow this rule: WHAT HAPPENS ON THE BIG SCREEN, SHOULD STAY ON THE BIG SCREEN.

BE THE PERSON THAT YOU THINK YOU SHOULD BE, NOT THE PERSON HOLLYWOOD ATTEMPTS TO INFLUENCE YOU TO BE!

Well, to be fair to the entertainment industry, I will say, that on the other side of the spectrum, there are some good natured, funny, uplifting and optimistic shows; that do connect with people, in positive ways.

Take for instance the Christian based movie; "Facing the Giants." I would really like it, if you, the reader, would watch this movie. Watch it, talk about it, and think about it. Films like this one, are just another way, that we can be reminded of God!

Be more concerned with your own character, than the characters you watch in the movies or on television. Remember, God is watching LIFE all day long, and you are one of LIFE'S characters!

--- C.W.

"We need people who influence their peers and who cannot be detoured from their convictions by peers who do not have the courage to have any convictions."

--- Joe Paterno(2)

"Character is what you are in the dark."

--- Dwight L. Moody(2)

Lesson 19.......... The Flow of Life

RULE: Stay on course!

If a natural water source is un-interrupted, the flow of water is constant, and can usually be seen running down its natural path of least resistance. For a human being, the flow of life is anything but easy and constant, as it follows many paths and/or courses.

When water hits rocks, or other objects, some of the water is displaced, but the flow of water will typically continue down its normal path. When people hit a small bump in life, their life may be altered a tad, yet, they too, are usually pretty good about staying on course. Most of the time, people are able to just go with the flow of things during their day to day lives, and are not really affected by much. They don't let the little things in life bug them. They just, "Go with the flow."

A person's course in life is somewhat complicated so we will keep it simple, and say that any course is a good course for a person, if that person wants to be on that course! Humans don't seek in one direction like water does; humans live life in a multi-directional way. Humans don't usually run up against actual rock-like walls that make them turn one way, or the other. With people, everything and everybody can impact a person's life, which may, or may not, affect whether or not a person stays on a given course. Some people end up taking a hard course, and doing things the hard way, while other people end up taking an easy course, and doing things the easy way. The course a person follows depends on a lot of things: preparation, proper planning, the right time, the right place; then there is dumb luck, and just how the ball bounces.

If water hits a giant boulder, it may take some time, but the water will seek out and find its natural path. If people hit a BIG Bump in life, such as divorce, loss of a job, hospital stay, jail time, or a personal situation, and they are thrown way off course, then it might take a period of time for them to get back to the life they want to have. The person who hits a BIG Bump in life will not automatically flow back to their intended path or adjust their course like water does. A person will have to come up with a plan of action to get back on course again. Friends and family are always a plus, but each individual person has to depend on, and look out for, himself or herself when planning a course of action.

Now you know! The natural flow of water is definitely a drop or two different than the flow of human life!

Be mindful, that you are the captain of your own ship. So, when plotting your course in this life, don't voluntarily steer yourself off course. It is hard to find direction in this life in a bottle of booze or while doing drugs. You cannot live life if you are lost in drugs and booze.

A Big Bump in life can pop up randomly and without warning, so be careful not to accidentally steer yourself toward one. Hitting a Big Bump in life, can make one lose their way in this life, but more than that, it can be a life stopper.

Generally speaking, people don't intentionally steer themselves toward Big Bumps, it just happens, when they do stupid things like....... doing drugs, drinking excessive alcohol, using tobacco products, texting while driving, not wearing a seatbelt, driving under the influence, not obeying all laws including the speed limit, not thinking before acting, and, well, quite frankly, by MAKING any other MISTAKES! By staying clear of the things that are on this list, you will be more able to safely navigate yourself through this life. One does not want to be shipwrecked and find themselves being a castaway from life.

I should tell you, that there is quite a big difference between just being a "little bit lost," and the kind of "lost," where you may never be able to find your way back.

Being a little bit lost will not land a person in jail, in the hospital or on the sidelines of life. Being a little bit lost, is not being the person that you want to be, or going down a course or path you don't want to be going down. The person who is a little bit lost is not living their best life.

Remember, in general, God gives us life, along with the ability to steer ourselves onto better courses. That way you can be all you want to be, and more importantly, all God wants you to be.

The path in life for each person is never the same; some paths are easy, and some are quite hard, but stay your course as best you can. You will always find your way back, using GOD as your COMPASS. Poor life, rich life, average life; just don't make it a lost life!

"It is a very bad thing to become accustomed to good luck."

------- Publilius Syrus (2)

"Let us throw off everything that hinders and the sin that so easily entangles, and let us run with perseverance the race marked out for us."

------- Hebrews 12:1(2)

5 P'S: "Proper Planning Prevents Poor Performance."

------- unknown

"If it is to be, it is up to me."

------- Frosty Westering (2)

THE EXCITEMENT MUST BE BUILDING UP BY NOW, BEING THAT WAS THE VERY LAST LESSON BEFORE GOING INTO GOD'S THEME PARK OF LIFE! I MEAN, YOU ARE SO CLOSE TO ENTERING THE THEME PARK, YOU CAN PROBABLY SMELL THE COTTON CANDY!!

SO, LIKE, WHAT ARE YOU STILL DOING HERE? SKEDADDLE!!!!! TURN THIS PAGE ALREADY, AND GET YOURSELF INTO GOD'S THEME PARK OF LIFE AS SOON AS POSSIBLE; NOW IS BETTER THAN LATER. GO! GO! GO!

GOD

I think I know what you are thinking! I'm thinking, that you are thinking, that this is a picture of God's Theme Park of Life. And if you are thinking, what I'm thinking, that you are thinking, then you shouldn't be thinking that, because this is only a picture of a typical, common, run of the mill, ordinary, amusement park. I guess in some way, this amusement park is kind of related to God's Theme Park of Life, but not really related; kind of a distant cousin type of a thing. But even looking at this picture, will most likely bring back wonderful memories of you and others smiling, laughing, and enjoying the rides!

BLESS

Well, since you are mentally in the wrong park, work your way to the nearest exit. Along the way be thinking that if this pictured park is typical, common, run of the mill, and ordinary, then God's Theme Park of Life must be atypical, un-common, completely unique, and extraordinary in every way imaginable.

When you exit this park by turning the page, you will find yourself at the Grand Entrance to God's Theme Park of Life! Prepare to be amazed! Are you ready...? Get set... Go!

EXIT →

YOU

**WELCOME TO PLANET EARTH,
OR WHAT I LIKE TO CALL
GOD'S THEME PARK OF LIFE!**

Keep your hands in, and your seatbelts buckled, because as crazy as it is, the entire human race is on one big ride.....called Planet Earth!

Planet Earth, or what I like to call GOD'S THEME PARK OF LIFE, is such a big park that anything and everything can happen. There are thrill rides, exciting rides, emotional rides, and the list of rides goes on and on. Everything you DO, TASTE, TOUCH, HEAR, SMELL, AND SEE, are considered rides in this park. Oh, before I forget to tell you, I was just kidding, about having to keep your hands in, and your seatbelts on. Once you free yourself, go have some fun in the park. In fact, go have a lot of fun!

Take trips down raging rivers, snorkel in tropical waters, hike in the beautiful outdoors listening to the wildlife as you go, taste foods from around the world, touch your spouse in loving ways, listen to the sounds of the ocean, smell the fragrance of orange blossoms, watch a thousand sunsets, and...........................

While you are in the park, there is really only one rule.

RULE: IF YOU START TO DO SOMETHING, WHEN YOU KNOW IT IS WRONG, THEN IT IS A SIN; SO, DON'T DO IT!

Stated yet, another way: IF YOU HAVE AN INKLING OF A THOUGHT THAT YOU SHOULDN'T GO ON A CERTAIN RIDE, THEN DON'T GO ON IT!

ANY SINNING DONE IN THE PARK WILL BE NOTED BY THE OWNER OF THE ESTABLISHMENT.

Since this is God's Theme Park, let's respect the one rule. Other than the one rule, HAVE THE TIME OF YOUR LIFE, BECAUSE IT IS YOUR LIFE!

Oh, one more thing I should mention; before the park closes, you are encouraged to go on the most amazing ride ever. The ride is called "The Leap of Faith," not to be confused with another ride called "The Leap of Fun."

"The Leap of Fun" is when a person, with a parachute, jumps out of a plane. "The Leap of Faith" is when a person, without a parachute, jumps into waiting hands.

"The Leap of Fun" is an exciting, adrenalin charged ride, and it begins when the side door to the airplane, that a rider is in, opens up, and the wind starts whirling around inside of the aircraft. The leaper steps to the open doorway, swaying back and forth in a nervous, excited, and animated type manner. The leaper leans forward, and lets go of whatever they were hanging onto, and… "ahhhhhhhhhhhh!!!!!!!!!"

The person is now free falling towards the ground; the rip cord is pulled, the chute opens up perfectly, and the person gives a sigh of relief. The subject lands safely on the ground, and the ride is over.

The ride was a blast! The only complaint the rider had was that sometime during the free fall experience, a wallet and a set of keys were lost.

When people talk about this ride, they say things like: "It scared me to death." "My life flashed before my eyes." "It scared the life right out of me."

A person is now standing in line, waiting for their turn to go on "The Leap of Faith!" The person has time to reflect back on their life so far. Some of it was good, some of it was bad, but for the most part it has been just fine. As the line gets shorter the person stops thinking about their own life, and starts thinking about a life with God. It is now the person's turn to go. The subject starts feeling excited, and then the adrenalin kicks in. The leaper leans forward, and lets go of whatever they were holding onto, and... ... nothing! No screaming, no fear of crashing to the ground, nothing, because as soon as the person took the "Leap of Faith" the subject landed instantaneously into God's hands! One thing that did happen was that a comforting feeling came over the person, a sense of inner peace. The leaper also gave a sigh of relief, like a big burden was lifted from their shoulders. The rider knew that everything was now going to be okay, because no matter what, God was always going to be there. Unlike other rides, this ride never ends!

The person on this ride also had a couple of things fall off. In fact, everyone on this ride always has the same things fall from them too. There are two things actually. One is worry, and the other is control issues, you know, those things that we can't control. Faith replaces them both.

When people talk about the "The Leap of Faith" they say things like: "This ride is life changing." "This ride is everlasting." "It's the best ride in the park!!"

"The Leap of Faith" also known as "Take the Leap," is open 24 hours a day, 7 days a week, and this book is a free pass to the front of the line. When you are ready, close your eyes...............or don't close your eyes. Let go of whatever you are hanging onto, give it all to God, and then............. "TAKE THE LEAP!!"

What I am kind of hoping for right now is that you will take some time to allow your mind to really absorb all of the many things that were in this book. Really put some thought into what you got out of the lessons, and how the "park pages" reminded you of the fact, that since your birth, you have always been in GOD'S THEME PARK OF LIFE!

After you have had some time, to think about all of those lessons, and all of those thoughts, both yours and mine, I am confident, that you will have a new, or renewed companionship with God. For those of you, who have always had a strong connection with God, I suspect, it will be much stronger.

Please feel free to review the lessons and quotes in this book. RELISH THE TIME, THAT YOU HAVE IN THE PARK!

ENJOY THE RIDE!

References

[1] Gotquestions.org

[2] 1001 Motivational Messages and Quotes, by Bruce Eamon Brown, © 2001 Coaches Choice.

[3] New Living Translation Bible, © 1996 Tyndale House Publishers Inc.

[**] Wikipedia The Free Encyclopedia; http//en.wikipedia.org and other internet websites were used to collect facts and figures for this book.

May the light be with you!

A Note About Me: The Author.

I was born, baptized, and raised as a Catholic. I consider myself to be a bench player in the Catholic Church, but I am an active player regarding my faith in God.

I am a Washington State University alumnus. Once a school teacher, but I have made a career out of being a Deputy Sheriff. My family and I reside in Washington State. Being a first-time author is quite exciting, and I found this avenue to be a great forum to express my views and thoughts regarding life and God.

This book would be a perfect gift for the Christmas season, or make it a gift for any reason. This book is available on-line at various locations, such as www.buybooksontheweb.com and Amazon.com.

CPSIA information can be obtained
at www.ICGtesting.com
Printed in the USA
FSHW02n0743080918

9 781495 820892